SCRATCH & PLAY

SCRIPPS NATIONAL SPELLING BEE

PUZZLE WRIGHT PRESS

New York

PUZZLE
WRIGHT
PRESS
New York

An Imprint of Sterling Publishing Co., Inc.
1166 Avenue of the Americas
New York, NY 10036

PUZZLEWRIGHT PRESS and the distinctive Puzzlewright Press logo
are registered trademarks of Sterling Publishing Co., Inc.

ISBN 978-1-4549-2251-3

Distributed in Canada by Sterling Publishing Co., Inc.
^{c}/o Canadian Manda Group, 664 Annette Street
Toronto, Ontario, Canada M6S 2C8
Distributed in the United Kingdom by GMC Distribution Services
Castle Place, 166 High Street, Lewes, East Sussex, England BN7 1XU
Distributed in Australia by NewSouth Books
45 Beach Street, Coogee, NSW 2034, Australia

For information about custom editions, special sales,
and premium and corporate purchases, please contact
Sterling Special Sales at 800-805-5489 or
specialsales@sterlingpublishing.com

Manufactured in China

2   4   6   8   10   9   7   5   3   1

sterlingpublishing.com
puzzlewright.com

Introduction

What's the buzz about "Scratch & Play Scripps National Spelling Bee"? Each word in this book was hand-selected by the team behind the Scripps National Spelling Bee with the goals of improving your spelling and increasing your vocabulary, and making you feel like the champion of the English language that you are.

This book, like a spelling bee, is meant to advance in difficulty as you work your way through it. Words 1–70 are a good place to start (we'll call them "easy," but they provide plenty of challenge); words 71–150 are medium difficulty; and, if you want to get straight to brain-busters and tongue twisters, you can skip straight to word 151. Words 151–250 are hard, intended to stretch your mind and impress your friends with sneaky hidden letters, useful roots, and fascinating origins.

Your mission is to scratch your way through each of the 250 words—maybe spelling aloud, with a friend, or on the page—and check each answer by scratching off the silver oval beneath the word information.

By including both diacritical and phonetic pronunciations for each word, this book will also help you increase fluency in reading the dictionary. These symbols may be strange at first, but treat them like a code and you'll have some fun. To get you started in cracking that code, we've provided this pronunciation key.

Pronunciation Key

ə = fun, alive	ī = fly, alive
ȧ = can be pronounced as	ŋ = long, ring
ə or i	ō = no, beau
a = apple, sat	ȯ = paw, bought
ā = name, day	ȯi = toy, poison
ä = bob, mall	sh = fish, shop
ch = child, rich	th = both, think
e = bend, cell	t̲h̲ = them, rather
ē = feet, each	u̇ = pull, push
ᵊ = little, mitten	ü = boo, ruby
i = mix, gym	zh = leisure, Asia

1.

Diacritical pronunciation: \ 'defənətlē \
Phonetic pronunciation: DEF-uh-nit-lee
Word origin: The first part of this word is from an originally Latin word, and the second part is an English combining form.
Part of speech: adverb
Definition: unmistakably or positively.
Example sentence: *Sarah told Angel that she will ~ go to the dance, even if she goes alone.*

2.

Diacritical pronunciation: \ 'kaləndər \
Phonetic pronunciation: KAL-in-dur
Word origin: This word is from an element from Latin or Anglo-French that became English.
Part of speech: noun
Definition: a list of dates and details of planned events.
Example sentence: *The college ~ begins with First Year Orientation Week.*

3.

Diacritical pronunciation: \ 'prin(t)səpəl \
Phonetic pronunciation: PRINT-suh-pul
Word origin: This word is from Latin.
Part of speech: noun
Definition: the official head of a school.
Example sentence: *After his experiment with breath mints and diet cola, Brad's teacher sent him to see the ~.*

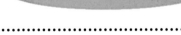

4.

Diacritical pronunciation: \ 'sepərət \
Phonetic pronunciation: SEP-uh-rit
Word origin: This word is from Latin.
Part of speech: adjective
Definition: set apart.
Example sentence: *The tour guide explained why the kitchen was usually a ~ building in colonial days.*

5.

Diacritical pronunciation: \ ˈrestəˌränt \

Phonetic pronunciation: RES-tuh-rahnt

Word origin: This word came from French, which formed it from a Latin word.

Part of speech: noun

Definition: a business where people can purchase and eat meals.

Example sentence: *Health inspectors visited the ~ three times before they would allow it to reopen.*

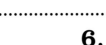

6.

Diacritical pronunciation: \ ˈfōrˌwərd \

Phonetic pronunciation: FOR-wurd

Word origin: This word consists of two originally English elements.

Part of speech: noun

Definition: front matter at the beginning of the book that is usually written by someone other than the author.

Example sentence: *The famous literary critic agreed to write a ~ to a collection of stories by Nobel Prize winners.*

7.

Diacritical pronunciation: \ ˈkapətᵊl \
Phonetic pronunciation: KAP-uh-tul
Word origin: This word is from Latin.
Part of speech: noun
Definition: a city serving as a seat for the government of a larger area.
Example sentence: *Alexander eagerly awaited his trip to the nation's ~.*

8.

Diacritical pronunciation: \ ˌkäntrəˈvərshəl \
Phonetic pronunciation: kahn-truh-VUR-shul
Word origin: This word is from Latin.
Part of speech: adjective
Definition: relating to or causing a dispute.
Example sentence: *The television show covers many hotly debated topics in its ~ new season.*

9.

Diacritical pronunciation: \ ˈmärshəl \
Phonetic pronunciation: MAHR-shul
Word origin: This word is from Latin.
Part of speech: adjective
Definition: relating to an army or to military life.
Example sentence: *Recruits need to acquire ~ skills before being assigned to a combat unit.*

10.

Diacritical pronunciation: \ ˈprivəlij \
Phonetic pronunciation: PRIV-uh-lij
Word origin: This word is from Latin.
Part of speech: noun
Definition: something granted as a benefit, advantage, or favor.
Example sentence: *Mr. Neng grants his neighbors the ~ of fishing in his pond.*

11.

Diacritical pronunciation: \ ik'sēd \
Phonetic pronunciation: ik-SEED
Word origin: This word came from French, which formed it from a Latin word.
Part of speech: verb
Definition: to be greater than or superior to.
Example sentence: *Mom makes a special treat each time the twins ~ her expectations on their report cards.*

12.

Diacritical pronunciation: \ 'despərət \
Phonetic pronunciation: DES-puh-rit
Word origin: This word is from Latin.
Part of speech: adjective
Definition: suffering extreme need or anxiety.
Example sentence: *By the end of the race, Beth was ~ for some water and a snack.*

13.

Diacritical pronunciation: \ sin'sirlē \
Phonetic pronunciation: sin-SEER-lee
Word origin: The first part of this word is from an originally Latin word, and the second part is an English combining form.
Part of speech: adverb
Definition: in a genuine manner.
Example sentence: *Tom ~ voiced profound remorse for how his actions had hurt his friends.*

14.

Diacritical pronunciation: \ ˈkäˌlēg \
Phonetic pronunciation: KAH-leeg
Word origin: This word came from French, which formed it from a Latin word.
Part of speech: noun
Definition: an associate or coworker typically of similar rank.
Example sentence: *After working late, Jenna and a ~ decided to go out to dinner.*

15.

Diacritical pronunciation: \ 'wenz(ˌ)dā \
Phonetic pronunciation: WENZ-day
Word origin: This word is originally English.
Part of speech: noun
Definition: the day following Tuesday.
Example sentence: *Many schoolchildren look forward to ~ as the day when the school week is half over.*

16.

Diacritical pronunciation: \ 'labrəˌtōrē \
Phonetic pronunciation: LAB-ruh-tor-ee
Word origin: This word is from Latin.
Part of speech: noun
Definition: a place devoted to experimental scientific study in testing and analysis or in the preparation of chemicals, explosives, or other products or substances.
Example sentence: *Matthew's parents are resisting his pleas to set up a ~ in the basement.*

17.

Diacritical pronunciation: \ prəˈspektiv \
Phonetic pronunciation: pruh-SPEK-tiv
Word origin: This word is from Latin.
Part of speech: adjective
Definition: of the future.
Example sentence: *The state requires that ~ teachers be certified before they begin serving in public schools.*

18.

Diacritical pronunciation: \ ˈsēliŋ \
Phonetic pronunciation: SEE-ling
Word origin: This word is originally English.
Part of speech: noun
Definition: the overhead surface of a room.
Example sentence: *The ~ of Danielle's room is covered with glow-in-the-dark stars.*

19.

Diacritical pronunciation: \ ˈfebrəˌwerē \
Phonetic pronunciation: FEB-ruh-wayr-ee
Word origin: This word is from Latin.
Part of speech: noun
Definition: the second month of the year.
Example sentence: *Kevin's car quit for good in ~.*

20.

Diacritical pronunciation: \ ˈsakrəˌfīs \
Phonetic pronunciation: SAK-ruh-fahys
Word origin: This word is from Latin.
Part of speech: noun
Definition: giving something up for a greater purpose.
Example sentence: *The commander commended the troops for their commitment and their ~.*

21.

Diacritical pronunciation: \ ˌpərsᵊn'el \
Phonetic pronunciation: pur-suh-NEL
Word origin: This word is from a word that went from Latin to German to French.
Part of speech: plural noun
Definition: individuals that make up a professional group.
Example sentence: *The secretary of defense called for a meeting with the highest-ranking military ~.*

22.

Diacritical pronunciation: \ 'iməˌgrāt \
Phonetic pronunciation: IM-uh-grayt
Word origin: This word is from Latin.
Part of speech: verb
Definition: come into a foreign country for the purpose of permanent residence.
Example sentence: *Individuals who ~ to the United States usually must wait years to become naturalized citizens.*

23.

Diacritical pronunciation: \ ˈkaǜn(t)səl \

Phonetic pronunciation: KAUNT-sul

Word origin: This word is from a Latin word that became French and then English.

Part of speech: noun

Definition: a lawyer engaged in a trial in a court.

Example sentence: *Gus waived his right to ~ and chose to represent himself in court.*

24.

Diacritical pronunciation: \ ˈparəˌlel \

Phonetic pronunciation: PAYR-uh-lel

Word origin: This word is from Greek.

Part of speech: adjective

Definition: extending in the same direction and equidistant at all points.

Example sentence: *Mr. Gordon's property extends back between ~ lines to a distance of 170 feet.*

25.

Diacritical pronunciation: \ ˈeləjəbəl \
Phonetic pronunciation: EL-i-juh-bul
Word origin: This word is from Latin.
Part of speech: adjective
Definition: qualified to be chosen or used.
Example sentence: *Tony must keep his grade point average at or above a C in order to remain ~ for the varsity tennis team.*

26.

Diacritical pronunciation: \ kənˈsen(t)səs \
Phonetic pronunciation: kun-SENT-sus
Word origin: This word is from Latin.
Part of speech: noun
Definition: collective opinion : the judgment arrived at by most of those concerned.
Example sentence: *The Booster Club's ~ was that popcorn would sell better than cotton candy.*

27.

Diacritical pronunciation: \ 'nälij \
Phonetic pronunciation: NAH-lij
Word origin: This word is originally English.
Part of speech: noun
Definition: understanding of an area of study or skills.
Example sentence: *Jack's ~ of carpentry immediately earned him a job when he arrived in Miami.*

28.

Diacritical pronunciation: \ 'disəplən \
Phonetic pronunciation: DIS-uh-plin
Word origin: This word came from French, which formed it from a Latin word.
Part of speech: noun
Definition: a subject or field of learning.
Example sentence: *Natasha's favorite ~ is European history of the seventeenth century.*

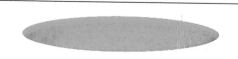

29.

Diacritical pronunciation: \ əˈkwit°l \

Phonetic pronunciation: uh-KWIT-ul

Word origin: This word consists of a Latin part plus a part that went from Latin to French.

Part of speech: noun

Definition: a setting free from the charge of an offense by verdict of a jury, sentence of a court, or other legal process.

Example sentence: *The prosecutor was less than thrilled when he received an invitation to the defendant's ~ pool party.*

30.

Diacritical pronunciation: \ ˈnōtəsəbəl \

Phonetic pronunciation: NO-tis-uh-bul

Word origin: This word consists of a part that went from Latin to French to English plus English combining forms.

Part of speech: adjective

Definition: capable of being observed.

Example sentence: *Dad's car makes a ~ banging noise when he drives faster than 70 miles per hour.*

31.

Diacritical pronunciation: \ əˈkərən(t)s \
Phonetic pronunciation: uh-KUR-unts
Word origin: This word came from French, which formed it from a Latin word.
Part of speech: noun
Definition: the action or process of happening or taking place.
Example sentence: *Willa prides herself on finding every ~ of a typographical error in her books.*

32.

Diacritical pronunciation: \ igˈzajəˌrāt \
Phonetic pronunciation: ig-ZAJ-uh-rayt
Word origin: This word is from Latin.
Part of speech: verb
Definition: to misrepresent on the side of largeness (as of size, extent, or value).
Example sentence: *Fishermen often ~ when describing the size of their catches.*

33.

Diacritical pronunciation: \ əˈkyümyəˌlāt \
Phonetic pronunciation: uh-KYOO-myuh-layt
Word origin: This word is from Latin.
Part of speech: verb
Definition: to grow or increase in quantity or number.
Example sentence: *The weather forecaster says that up to two feet of snow will likely ~ overnight.*

34.

Diacritical pronunciation: \ ˌəndərˈrātəd \
Phonetic pronunciation: un-dur-RAY-tid
Word origin: The first part of this word is an English combining form, and the second part is from an originally Latin word.
Part of speech: verb
Definition: valued too low.
Example sentence: *The students soon learned that they had ~ the intelligence of their teacher.*

35.

Diacritical pronunciation: \ ˌsakrəˈlijəs \
Phonetic pronunciation: sak-ruh-LIJ-us
Word origin: This word is from Latin.
Part of speech: adjective
Definition: involving irreverence toward a respected person, place, or thing.
Example sentence: *Gavin believes it's ~ to prefer Superman to Batman.*

36.

Diacritical pronunciation: \ ˈreləvənt \
Phonetic pronunciation: REL-uh-vunt
Word origin: This word is from Latin.
Part of speech: adjective
Definition: applying to the matter at hand.
Example sentence: *The defense attorney maintained that the information was ~ to the charges against his client.*

37.

Diacritical pronunciation: \ fak'siməlē \
Phonetic pronunciation: fak-SIM-uh-lee
Word origin: This word is from Latin.
Part of speech: noun
Definition: an exact and detailed copy of something (as of a book, document, painting, or statue).
Example sentence: *Jared bought a ~ of Noah Webster's 1828 dictionary.*

38.

Diacritical pronunciation: \ 'kämpləmənt \
Phonetic pronunciation: KAHM-pluh-munt
Word origin: This word is from Latin.
Part of speech: noun
Definition: a finishing part or component.
Example sentence: *The earrings are the perfect ~ to Anjali's ensemble.*

39.

Diacritical pronunciation: \ ˈstāshəˌnerē \
Phonetic pronunciation: STAY-shun-ayr-ee
Word origin: This word came from French, which formed it from a Latin word.
Part of speech: noun
Definition: writing materials such as paper, pens, pencils, and cards.
Example sentence: *Claudia, a frequent letter-writer, says her favorite place to shop is the ~ store.*

40.

Diacritical pronunciation: \ sīˈkäləjē \
Phonetic pronunciation: sahy-KAH-luh-jee
Word origin: This word is from originally Greek parts.
Part of speech: noun
Definition: the science of the mind or of mental phenomena and activities.
Example sentence: *Wilhelm Wundt is commonly considered the father of modern ~.*

41.

Diacritical pronunciation: \ 'vaˌkyüm \

Phonetic pronunciation: VAK-yoom

Word origin: This word is from Latin.

Part of speech: noun

Definition: a space devoid of air.

Example sentence: *Professor Benson switched on the pump to create a ~ in the tube through which the laser beam would travel.*

42.

Diacritical pronunciation: \ 'plāˌrīt \

Phonetic pronunciation: PLAY-rahyt

Word origin: This word consists of two originally English elements.

Part of speech: noun

Definition: a person who writes a work, usually with dialogue, for actors to enact on a stage.

Example sentence: *The ~ based his drama in part on the struggles between gangs in the city.*

43.

Diacritical pronunciation: \ ˌtemp(ə)rə'mentᵊl \
Phonetic pronunciation: temp-ur-uh-MEN-tul
Word origin: This word is from Latin.
Part of speech: adjective
Definition: excessively sensitive and impulsive, and subject to often explosive changes of mood.
Example sentence: *When the ~ player disputed the umpire's call, he was ejected from the game.*

44.

Diacritical pronunciation: \ 'sekrəˌterē \
Phonetic pronunciation: SEK-ruh-tayr-ee
Word origin: This word is from Latin.
Part of speech: noun
Definition: an officer of an organization or society responsible for its records.
Example sentence: *Jenna's father is ~ of the administrative board of her preschool.*

45.

Diacritical pronunciation: \ ˈmischəvəs \
Phonetic pronunciation: MIS-chi-vus
Word origin: This word is originally English.
Part of speech: adjective
Definition: tending to cause annoyance, trouble, or minor damage to others.
Example sentence: *Manny's ~ behavior got him grounded for a week.*

46.

Diacritical pronunciation: \ əmˈbarəs \
Phonetic pronunciation: im-BAYR-us
Word origin: This word is from a word that went from Portuguese to Spanish to French.
Part of speech: verb
Definition: to cause a state of self-consciousness.
Example sentence: *Rob's mother knows from experience that pointing out her son's dimples will ~ him.*

47.

Diacritical pronunciation: \ ˈkərn°l \
Phonetic pronunciation: KUR-nul
Word origin: This word is from a Latin word that became Italian and then French.
Part of speech: noun
Definition: a military officer ranking below a brigadier general.
Example sentence: *Jim was promoted to the rank of ~ in recognition of his achievements.*

48.

Diacritical pronunciation: \ ˈnȯshəs \
Phonetic pronunciation: NAH-shus
Word origin: This word is from Latin.
Part of speech: adjective
Definition: sickening or disgusting.
Example sentence: *The smell emanating from the swamp was ~.*

49.

Diacritical pronunciation: \ ˈseməˌterē \

Phonetic pronunciation: SEM-uh-tayr-ee

Word origin: This word is from an originally Greek word that passed into Latin and then French before becoming English.

Part of speech: noun

Definition: a burial ground or graveyard.

Example sentence: *Matthew got the creeps whenever he walked through the ~ on his way to Bruno's house.*

50.

Diacritical pronunciation: \ iˈnäkyəwəs \

Phonetic pronunciation: i-NAH-kyuh-wus

Word origin: This word is from Latin.

Part of speech: adjective

Definition: inoffensive.

Example sentence: *Betty was dismayed when Henry interpreted her ~ remark as an insult.*

51.

Diacritical pronunciation: \ yü'nanəməs \
Phonetic pronunciation: yoo-NAN-uh-mus
Word origin: This word is from Latin.
Part of speech: adjective
Definition: agreeing in opinion.
Example sentence: *Having expected at least some opposition, Leandra was surprised by the ~ decision to name her head cheerleader.*

52.

Diacritical pronunciation: \ bī'anyəwəl \
Phonetic pronunciation: bahy-AN-yuh-wul
Word origin: This word consists of Latin-derived elements.
Part of speech: adjective
Definition: happening twice a year.
Example sentence: *Because the company's president felt that its yearly review of sales was not frequent enough, he decided to make the evaluation a ~ event.*

53.

Diacritical pronunciation: \ əˈkäməˌdāt \
Phonetic pronunciation: uh-KAH-muh-dayt
Word origin: This word is from Latin.
Part of speech: verb
Definition: provide with a place to stay.
Example sentence: *Arthur insisted on staying in a hotel that would ~ Paco, his elderly Chihuahua.*

54.

Diacritical pronunciation: \ igˈziləˌrāt \
Phonetic pronunciation: ig-ZIL-uh-rayt
Word origin: This word is from Latin.
Part of speech: verb
Definition: to refresh or invigorate.
Example sentence: *The end-of-year celebration will ~ students and teachers alike.*

55.

Diacritical pronunciation: \ ˈrithəm \

Phonetic pronunciation: RITH-um

Word origin: This word is from an originally Greek word that passed into Latin and then French.

Part of speech: noun

Definition: the pattern and succession of beats in music.

Example sentence: *Latin American music is usually easily recognizable by its distinctive ~.*

56.

Diacritical pronunciation: \ ˈse(ˌ)gwā \

Phonetic pronunciation: SEG-way

Word origin: This word came from Italian, which formed it from a Latin word.

Part of speech: verb

Definition: to make a transition from one activity, topic, scene, or part to another.

Example sentence: *Senator Ward will ~ to a new topic in his speech with an anecdote.*

57.

Diacritical pronunciation: \ lü'tenənt \

Phonetic pronunciation: loo-TEN-unt

Word origin: This word came from French, which formed it from a Latin word.

Part of speech: noun

Definition: a commissioned officer in the army, navy, air force, or marine corps.

Example sentence: *At the end of the novel, the young infantry hero was finally promoted to ~.*

58.

Diacritical pronunciation: \ ˌbenə'fishēˌerē \

Phonetic pronunciation: ben-uh-FISH-ee-ayr-ee

Word origin: This word is from Latin.

Part of speech: noun

Definition: the person named (as in an insurance or annuity policy) as the one who is to receive payments.

Example sentence: *Cora named her son as the ~ of her life insurance policy.*

59.

Diacritical pronunciation: \ ˈaməˌchu̇r \
Phonetic pronunciation: AM-uh-choor
Word origin: This word came from French, which formed it from a Latin word.
Part of speech: noun
Definition: a person who participates in a study or activity as a pastime rather than as a profession.
Example sentence: *Although Rosalind is excellent for an ~, she refuses to enter chess tournaments.*

60.

Diacritical pronunciation: \ byu̇ˈräkrəsē \
Phonetic pronunciation: byoo-RAH-kruh-see
Word origin: This word is from a French word plus a Greek-derived element.
Part of speech: noun
Definition: a particular group of government officials.
Example sentence: *Bennett quickly moved up in the ~ of the Justice Department.*

61.

Diacritical pronunciation: \ iˈnäkyəˌlāt \

Phonetic pronunciation: i-NAH-kyuh-layt

Word origin: This word is from a word that went from Latin to English.

Part of speech: verb

Definition: to treat with microorganisms or vaccines in order to establish immunity to a disease.

Example sentence: *Dr. Cooper knows that she will only be able to ~ Colin if she bribes him with a lollipop.*

62.

Diacritical pronunciation: \ pəˈzeshən \

Phonetic pronunciation: puh-ZESH-un

Word origin: This word went from Latin through French to English.

Part of speech: noun

Definition: something that is owned.

Example sentence: *Mallory's prized ~ is a stuffed unicorn with a rainbow mane.*

63.

Diacritical pronunciation: \ ˈsatᵊlˌīt \
Phonetic pronunciation: SAT-uh-lahyt
Word origin: This word is from a probably Etruscan-derived Latin word.
Part of speech: noun
Definition: a celestial body orbiting another of larger size.
Example sentence: *Earth has only one natural ~: the Moon.*

64.

Diacritical pronunciation: \ ˈkash \
Phonetic pronunciation: kash
Word origin: This word came from French, which formed it from a Latin word.
Part of speech: noun
Definition: a hiding place.
Example sentence: *Captain Jack buried a ~ of stolen treasure under a lone palm tree.*

65.

Diacritical pronunciation: \ priˈkōshəs \
Phonetic pronunciation: pri-KOH-shus
Word origin: This word is from Latin.
Part of speech: adjective
Definition: developing mentally or physically very early.
Example sentence: *What Paula at first took to be Quinn's ~ interest in dance turned out to be his way of telling her he needed a diaper change.*

66.

Diacritical pronunciation: \ ˌkȯrəˈspändən(t)s \
Phonetic pronunciation: kor-uh-SPAHN-dunts
Word origin: This word came from French, which formed it from a Latin word.
Part of speech: noun
Definition: messages exchanged between people.
Example sentence: *Looking for previously unknown information, the biographer read through his subject's ~.*

67.

Diacritical pronunciation: \ lēˈāˌzän \
Phonetic pronunciation: lee-AY-zahn
Word origin: This word is from a French word.
Part of speech: noun
Definition: any intercommunication for establishing and maintaining mutual understanding.
Example sentence: *~ is essential in coordinating local and state police activities.*

68.

Diacritical pronunciation: \ ˈkän(t)shēˌen(t)shəs \
Phonetic pronunciation: KAHNT-shee-ent-shus
Word origin: This word is from Latin.
Part of speech: adjective
Definition: made according to the sense of right or wrong : honest.
Example sentence: *Janice was very ~ about telling the truth.*

69.

Diacritical pronunciation: \ məˈlenēəm \
Phonetic pronunciation: muh-LEN-ee-um
Word origin: This word is from Latin.
Part of speech: noun
Definition: a period of 1,000 years.
Example sentence: *Although it really only took her about three hours, Tori was sure it would take her about a ~ to clean her room.*

70.

Diacritical pronunciation: \ ˈgamət \
Phonetic pronunciation: GAM-ut
Word origin: This word is probably from an originally Greek word that passed into Latin.
Part of speech: noun
Definition: an entire range from one extreme to another.
Example sentence: *The products unveiled at the auto show ran the ~ from hybrid vehicles to sporty race cars.*

71.

Diacritical pronunciation: \ ˌēkwəˈlibrəst \
Phonetic pronunciation: ee-kwuh-LIB-rist
Word origin: This word came from French, which formed it from a Latin word.
Part of speech: noun
Definition: an acrobat skilled at balancing in dangerous positions.
Example sentence: *Of all the acts in the circus, Yancy liked the ~ best.*

72.

Diacritical pronunciation: \ ˈȯfəl \
Phonetic pronunciation: AH-ful
Word origin: This word is from English.
Part of speech: noun
Definition: the entrails and internal organs of a butchered animal.
Example sentence: *A growing number of innovative American chefs are incorporating ~ into everyday menus.*

73.

Diacritical pronunciation: \ prē'nəpshəl \

Phonetic pronunciation: pree-NUP-shul

Word origin: This word is from a Latin-derived English combining form plus a Latin-derived element.

Part of speech: adjective

Definition: leading up to marriage.

Example sentence: *Marlo gained three pounds during the month of ~ parties.*

74.

Diacritical pronunciation: \ kə'mikschər \

Phonetic pronunciation: kuh-MIKS-chur

Word origin: This word is from Latin.

Part of speech: noun

Definition: the result of mixing things together.

Example sentence: *Henry's art project was best described as a ~ of glue, nails, and cardboard.*

75.

Diacritical pronunciation: \ ˈfərbə͵lō \

Phonetic pronunciation: FUR-buh-loh

Word origin: This word is from a French word that then became English.

Part of speech: noun

Definition: a ruffle or flounce on clothing.

Example sentence: *Delia sewed a ~ to the hem of her skirt.*

76.

Diacritical pronunciation: \ ˈrərbən \

Phonetic pronunciation: RUR-bun

Word origin: This word is a blend of two Latin-derived words.

Part of speech: adjective

Definition: not in the city but not on a farm.

Example sentence: *Pauline grew up in a ~ environment but moved to the city as soon as she could.*

77.

Diacritical pronunciation: \ ˌyükəˈliptəs \
Phonetic pronunciation: yoo-kuh-LIP-tus
Word origin: This word is from originally Greek parts.
Part of speech: noun
Definition: an Australian evergreen tree that yields gums, resins, and oils.
Example sentence: *The ~ is the koala's main source of food.*

78.

Diacritical pronunciation: \ kriˈpəskyələr \
Phonetic pronunciation: kri-PUS-kyuh-lur
Word origin: The first part of this word is from an originally Latin word, and the second part is an English combining form.
Part of speech: adjective
Definition: active in the twilight.
Example sentence: *Darnel answered "firefly" when the teacher asked for an example of a ~ insect.*

79.

Diacritical pronunciation: \ ˌabəˈrāshən \
Phonetic pronunciation: ab-uh-RAY-shun
Word origin: This word is from Latin.
Part of speech: noun
Definition: an act or instance that is different from the norm.
Example sentence: *Jane's outburst at the meeting was a shocking behavioral ~, since she is usually very reserved.*

80.

Diacritical pronunciation: \ ˈrekrēənt \
Phonetic pronunciation: REK-ree-unt
Word origin: Originally Latin, this word went through French before becoming English.
Part of speech: noun
Definition: a deserter.
Example sentence: *The girls called Nika a ~ after she ditched the One Direction fan club for the Zayn Malik fan club.*

81.

Diacritical pronunciation: \ ˈmäbəˌkrat \
Phonetic pronunciation: MAH-buh-krat
Word origin: This word is from an originally Latin part plus a part that went from Greek to Latin.
Part of speech: noun
Definition: a person who believes in the rule of the masses.
Example sentence: *The revolutionary Samuel Adams was considered a ~ by the British colonial governor of Massachusetts.*

82.

Diacritical pronunciation: \ ˈfēkənd \
Phonetic pronunciation: FEE-kund
Word origin: This word is from Latin.
Part of speech: adjective
Definition: intellectually productive and inventive.
Example sentence: *The Renaissance was a ~ era for the arts.*

83.

Diacritical pronunciation: \ ˈventrəkəl \

Phonetic pronunciation: VEN-tri-kul

Word origin: This word is from Latin.

Part of speech: noun

Definition: a chamber of the heart that receives blood from an atrium and sends blood into the arteries.

Example sentence: *The heart patient's right ~ is the source of his trouble.*

84.

Diacritical pronunciation: \ paˈvlōvə \

Phonetic pronunciation: pa-VLOH-vuh

Word origin: This word is from a Russian name.

Part of speech: noun

Definition: a meringue shell topped with whipped cream and fruit eaten as a dessert.

Example sentence: *~ is most often served during celebratory and holiday meals in Australia and New Zealand.*

85.

Diacritical pronunciation: \ ek'skäjə₁tāt \
Phonetic pronunciation: ek-SKAH-juh-tayt
Word origin: This word is from Latin.
Part of speech: verb
Definition: to thoroughly and carefully think through.
Example sentence: *Lindsay will ~ the topic completely and outline his thoughts before he begins writing his report.*

86.

Diacritical pronunciation: \ ₁desəl'tōrəlē \
Phonetic pronunciation: des-ul-TOR-uh-lee
Word origin: This word is from Latin.
Part of speech: adverb
Definition: in an erratic, wavering manner.
Example sentence: *Flags fluttered ~ in the strong breeze.*

87.

Diacritical pronunciation: \ shiˈfän \

Phonetic pronunciation: shi-FAHN

Word origin: This word came to English from French, which took it from an originally English word.

Part of speech: noun

Definition: a sheer, lightweight fabric with a soft finish.

Example sentence: *The singer sauntered into the spotlight in a dress of white ~.*

88.

Diacritical pronunciation: \ ˈflagən \

Phonetic pronunciation: FLAG-un

Word origin: Perhaps originally Germanic, this word passed through Latin and French before becoming English.

Part of speech: noun

Definition: a large vessel for holding liquid that has a handle and spout and often a lid.

Example sentence: *The ~ on Mrs. Wilburn's mantel was made in England by a famous pewtersmith.*

89.

Diacritical pronunciation: \ ˈnarēəl \
Phonetic pronunciation: NAYR-ee-ul
Word origin: This word is from Latin.
Part of speech: adjective
Definition: related to the nostrils.
Example sentence: *There are several different sorts of septa, but perhaps the best known is the ~ septum.*

90.

Diacritical pronunciation: \ ˈstelyələr \
Phonetic pronunciation: STEL-yuh-lur
Word origin: This word is from Latin.
Part of speech: adjective
Definition: shaped like a small star.
Example sentence: *For each grammatical error in the essay the teacher placed a ~ mark in the margin.*

91.

Diacritical pronunciation: \ ˈkȯrēˌandər \

Phonetic pronunciation: KOR-ee-an-dur

Word origin: Originally Greek, this word went through Latin and French before becoming English.

Part of speech: noun

Definition: an herb whose leaves are used fresh and fruits are used dried in cooking.

Example sentence: *Jane almost always uses ~ to season her stew.*

92.

Diacritical pronunciation: \ əˌklīmətəˈzāshən \

Phonetic pronunciation: uh-klahy-muh-tuh-ZAY-shun

Word origin: The first part of this word was originally Latin and then became French, and the remaining parts are English combining forms.

Part of speech: noun

Definition: the act of adjusting to a new environment.

Example sentence: *The wild fern's ~ to Mrs. Bennett's rock garden amazed her.*

93.

Diacritical pronunciation: \ (ˌ)kər'məjən \
Phonetic pronunciation: kur-MUH-jun
Word origin: This word is of unknown origin.
Part of speech: noun
Definition: an unpleasant or difficult person.
Example sentence: *The ~ criticized the book as having too many pages between the covers.*

94.

Diacritical pronunciation: \ ˌfēlə'sifik \
Phonetic pronunciation: fee-luh-SIF-ik
Word origin: This word is from Latin.
Part of speech: adjective
Definition: producing happiness.
Example sentence: *Robert longed for a ~ conclusion to his job application experience.*

95.

Diacritical pronunciation: \ ˈtärməgən \
Phonetic pronunciation: TAHR-mi-gun
Word origin: This word is a modification of an originally Scottish Gaelic word.
Part of speech: noun
Definition: any of various grouses of northern regions with completely feathered feet.
Example sentence: *The white-tailed ~ has feathers on its feet to help keep it from sinking in the snow.*

96.

Diacritical pronunciation: \ riˈsəsəˌtāt \
Phonetic pronunciation: ri-SUS-uh-tayt
Word origin: This word is from Latin.
Part of speech: verb
Definition: to revive.
Example sentence: *Jenna peeked ahead to the last chapter of the book and learned that a young hospital intern would ~ the main character.*

97.

Diacritical pronunciation: \ ˈkrasəˌtüd \
Phonetic pronunciation: KRAS-uh-tood
Word origin: This word is from Latin.
Part of speech: noun
Definition: the quality of being gross or unfeeling.
Example sentence: *The main character's extreme ~ overshadowed the movie's clever plot.*

98.

Diacritical pronunciation: \ ˌəngetˈatəbəl \
Phonetic pronunciation: un-get-AT-uh-bul
Word origin: This word is made up of English elements.
Part of speech: adjective
Definition: inaccessible.
Example sentence: *Dad declared that the Legos under the refrigerator were ~.*

99.

Diacritical pronunciation: \ əˈprōbrēəs \

Phonetic pronunciation: uh-PROH-bree-us

Word origin: Originally Latin, this word went through French before becoming English.

Part of speech: adjective

Definition: expressive of contempt, reproach, and an implication of inferiority.

Example sentence: *The principal denounced the vandals in ~ terms.*

100.

Diacritical pronunciation: \ əˈnīəˌlāt \

Phonetic pronunciation: uh-NAHY-uh-layt

Word origin: This word is from Latin.

Part of speech: verb

Definition: to get rid of completely.

Example sentence: *An infestation of armyworms can ~ a beautiful lawn in just a few days.*

101.

Diacritical pronunciation: \ bī'sektər \
Phonetic pronunciation: bahy-SEK-tur
Word origin: This word is from Latin.
Part of speech: noun
Definition: a straight line dividing an angle or a line segment into two parts.
Example sentence: *Wolfe drew the ~ using only a compass and a straightedge.*

102.

Diacritical pronunciation: \ 'disənən(t)s \
Phonetic pronunciation: DIS-uh-nun(t)s
Word origin: This word is from Latin.
Part of speech: noun
Definition: an arrangement of clashing sounds.
Example sentence: *The composer relied on ~ to express the tension in a particular passage.*

103.

Diacritical pronunciation: \ məˈtastəˌsīz \
Phonetic pronunciation: mi-TAS-tuh-sahyz
Word origin: This word is from Greek.
Part of speech: verb
Definition: to spread from an original site of disease to another part of the body.
Example sentence: *The oncologist pointed on the drawing to where he believes the cancer cells will ~ next.*

104.

Diacritical pronunciation: \ pyüˈtresᵊnt \
Phonetic pronunciation: pyoo-TRES-unt
Word origin: This word is from Latin.
Part of speech: adjective
Definition: decaying or rotting.
Example sentence: *Finney was surprised to find that the compost pile didn't have a ~ odor at all.*

105.

Diacritical pronunciation: \ səˈbòltərn \
Phonetic pronunciation: suh-BAHL-turn
Word origin: This word is from Latin.
Part of speech: adjective
Definition: inferior.
Example sentence: *Julie had heard the Stanislavski quote "There are no small parts, only small actors," but it was no consolation when she received her ~ role as Fish #4 in "The Little Mermaid."*

106.

Diacritical pronunciation: \ īˈdilik \
Phonetic pronunciation: ahy-DIL-ik
Word origin: This word is from Greek.
Part of speech: adjective
Definition: peaceful, pleasing, or picturesque due to natural simplicity.
Example sentence: *The Elsons spent a week in an ~ little town in the Pyrenees.*

107.

Diacritical pronunciation: \ ˈsībərˌnȯt \

Phonetic pronunciation: SAHY-bur-naht

Word origin: This word is made up of two originally Greek parts.

Part of speech: noun

Definition: someone who is active in the internet community.

Example sentence: *Mario could hardly believe that his niece was an experienced ~ at the ripe old age of seven.*

108.

Diacritical pronunciation: \ hiˌstōrēˈet \

Phonetic pronunciation: hi-stor-ee-ET

Word origin: This word is from a word that went from Greek to Latin to French plus a French combining form.

Part of speech: noun

Definition: a short written narrative including a chronological record of events.

Example sentence: *Marla earned an A on her ~ of her great-grandfather's life.*

109.

Diacritical pronunciation: \ ˌlögə'pēdiks \
Phonetic pronunciation: lahg-uh-PEE-diks
Word origin: This word is made up of originally Greek parts.
Part of speech: plural noun
Definition: the scientific study and treatment of speech defects.
Example sentence: *Many children with speech defects have been successfully treated at a center for ~.*

110.

Diacritical pronunciation: \ ˌkyùrē'ō(ˌ)sō \
Phonetic pronunciation: kyoor-ee-OH-soh
Word origin: This word is from Italian, which formed it from a Latin word.
Part of speech: noun
Definition: a collector of rarities or articles of artistic worth.
Example sentence: *Amelia is considered a ~ for her large collection of neo-Egyptian jewelry.*

111.

Diacritical pronunciation: \ ˌjēnēəˈläjəkəl \

Phonetic pronunciation: jee-nee-uh-LAH-jik-ul

Word origin: This word is from Greek.

Part of speech: adjective

Definition: relating to a listing of ancestors and their descendants in order.

Example sentence: *A family tree is a representation of ~ relationships.*

112.

Diacritical pronunciation: \ ˈrivyələt \

Phonetic pronunciation: RIV-yuh-lit

Word origin: This word is from Greek.

Part of speech: noun

Definition: a small stream.

Example sentence: *The water from the fast-melting snow gushed down the ~ to the pond below.*

113.

Diacritical pronunciation: \ ek'säjənəs \
Phonetic pronunciation: ek-SAH-juh-nus
Word origin: This word consists of two Greek-derived elements that passed into French plus an English combining form.
Part of speech: adjective
Definition: coming from external causes.
Example sentence: *The politician argued that the labor strife in his city was ~ in nature.*

114.

Diacritical pronunciation: \ 'demē₁ərj \
Phonetic pronunciation: DEM-ee-urj
Word origin: This word is from an originally Greek word that passed into Latin.
Part of speech: noun
Definition: an institution, idea, or person acting as a self-contained creative force or decisive power.
Example sentence: *It is surprising how many people tend to regard a computer as a ~.*

115.

Diacritical pronunciation: \ ˌbaləˈtäzh \
Phonetic pronunciation: bal-uh-TAZH
Word origin: This word is from a French word.
Part of speech: noun
Definition: a second vote taken to decide the winner when no candidate receives a majority in the first vote.
Example sentence: *In the United States a ~ is usually called a "runoff election."*

116.

Diacritical pronunciation: \ ˈrübəkənd \
Phonetic pronunciation: ROO-bi-kund
Word origin: This word is from Latin.
Part of speech: adjective
Definition: ruddy or reddish.
Example sentence: *Callie's face is always ~ and dry after walking to work on a windy winter day.*

117.

Diacritical pronunciation: \ səbˈləkˌsātəd \
Phonetic pronunciation: sub-LUK-say-tid
Word origin: This word is from Latin.
Part of speech: adjective
Definition: partially dislocated, as of a joint.
Example sentence: *The chiropractor told Tara that her cervical vertebrae were probably ~ as a result of the car accident she had been in three years earlier.*

118.

Diacritical pronunciation: \ īˈsänəmē \
Phonetic pronunciation: ahy-SAH-nuh-mee
Word origin: This word is originally Greek.
Part of speech: noun
Definition: equality under the law.
Example sentence: *The candidate preached ~ for all citizens, though he suggested that some ought to have more ~ than others.*

119.

Diacritical pronunciation: \ sē'nägrəfər \
Phonetic pronunciation: see-NAH-gruh-fur
Word origin: This word is from Greek.
Part of speech: noun
Definition: a person who applies perspective representation in painting stage scenery.
Example sentence: *The ~ painted a mountainous background for a setting of "The Sound of Music."*

120.

Diacritical pronunciation: \ 'flòrəwət \
Phonetic pronunciation: FLOR-uh-wit
Word origin: This word is from Latin.
Part of speech: noun
Definition: a period during which something thrived most.
Example sentence: *Professor Snodgrass explained that when we don't know the birth and death dates of an ancient author, we often still know a ~.*

121.

Diacritical pronunciation: \ ˌserəˈbelər \
Phonetic pronunciation: sayr-uh-BEL-ur
Word origin: This word is from Latin.
Part of speech: adjective
Definition: relating to the large part of the brain that coordinates muscles and maintains equilibrium.
Example sentence: ~ *diseases often cause disturbances in gait and balance.*

122.

Diacritical pronunciation: \ ˌaməˈriləs \
Phonetic pronunciation: am-uh-RIL-is
Word origin: This word is probably from a Latin name.
Part of speech: noun
Definition: a flowering bulb originally from southern Africa.
Example sentence: *Deborah's ~ bloomed just in time for the December holidays.*

123.

Diacritical pronunciation: \ yü'theniks \
Phonetic pronunciation: yoo-THEN-iks
Word origin: This word is from Greek parts plus an English combining form.
Part of speech: plural noun
Definition: a science that deals with improving human life by bettering environmental conditions.
Example sentence: *As the world becomes more populated, people pay more attention to the relevance of ~.*

124.

Diacritical pronunciation: \ ˌikthē'äləjē \
Phonetic pronunciation: ik-thee-AH-luh-jee
Word origin: This word is from originally Greek parts.
Part of speech: noun
Definition: the scientific study of fishes.
Example sentence: *Mr. Pout didn't need a degree in ~ to see that he had caught a dead branch.*

125.

Diacritical pronunciation: \ (ˌ)kwinsen'tenərē \
Phonetic pronunciation: kwin-sen-TEN-uh-ree
Word origin: This word is from originally Latin parts.
Part of speech: noun
Definition: a 500th anniversary.
Example sentence: *The Lutheran Church celebrated its ~ in 2017.*

126.

Diacritical pronunciation: \ sep'tarēəm \
Phonetic pronunciation: sep-TAYR-ee-um
Word origin: This word is from Latin.
Part of speech: noun
Definition: a lump of limestone or clay ironstone containing cracks filled with other minerals.
Example sentence: *When Benjamin found a very smooth round rock, he sawed it in half to find out if it was a ~.*

127.

Diacritical pronunciation: \ ˈvōlərē \
Phonetic pronunciation: VOH-lur-ee
Word origin: This word is made up of a Latin element and an English combining form.
Part of speech: noun
Definition: the birds in an enclosure.
Example sentence: *The zoo has collected an exotic ~ from South America.*

128.

Diacritical pronunciation: \ ˌmȯrəˈtōrēəm \
Phonetic pronunciation: mor-uh-TOR-ee-um
Word origin: This word is from Latin.
Part of speech: noun
Definition: a waiting period required by an authority.
Example sentence: *Until the feathers were all cleaned up, they washed the maple syrup off their hands, and grandma had gone to bed, mom put a ~ on pillow fights.*

129.

Diacritical pronunciation: \ ˌrēkrüˈdesᵊn(t)s \
Phonetic pronunciation: ree-kroo-DES-un(t)s
Word origin: This word is from Latin.
Part of speech: noun
Definition: an unwelcome or undesirable renewal.
Example sentence: *Tabitha baked her neighbors two pans of brownies and wrote a lengthy apology note in an attempt to avoid a ~ of hostile feelings after the most recent casserole incident.*

130.

Diacritical pronunciation: \ siˈkwelə \
Phonetic pronunciation: si-KWEL-uh
Word origin: This word is from Latin.
Part of speech: noun
Definition: an aftereffect or consequence.
Example sentence: *Thinking "Why don't they just say aftereffect?" is a common ~ of learning what ~ means.*

131.

Diacritical pronunciation: \ dəsˈriᴛʜmēə \
Phonetic pronunciation: dis-RITH-mee-uh
Word origin: This word consists of two originally Greek parts that passed into Latin.
Part of speech: noun
Definition: jet lag.
Example sentence: *The travel agent gave the tour group several tips on how to avoid ~.*

132.

Diacritical pronunciation: \ ˈbrōg \
Phonetic pronunciation: brohg
Word origin: This word is perhaps from Irish Gaelic.
Part of speech: noun
Definition: an Irish accent.
Example sentence: *The leprechaun spoke with a charming ~.*

133.

Diacritical pronunciation: \ kənˈkämətən(t)s \
Phonetic pronunciation: kun-KAH-muh-tun(t)s
Word origin: This word is from Latin.
Part of speech: noun
Definition: an occurrence of something at the same time as something else.
Example sentence: *Cybelle commented on the conspicuous ~ of poverty and wealth in the city center.*

134.

Diacritical pronunciation: \ ˈkrisəˌlīt \
Phonetic pronunciation: KRIS-uh-lahyt
Word origin: This word went from Greek to Latin to French to English.
Part of speech: noun
Definition: any of several yellow or greenish gems.
Example sentence: *The mysterious woman had a beautifully cut ~ set into her ring.*

135.

Diacritical pronunciation: \ ˈjüdō͵kä \
Phonetic pronunciation: JOO-doh-kah
Word origin: This word is from Japanese.
Part of speech: noun
Definition: a practitioner of a form of jujitsu utilizing principles of movement, balance, and leverage.
Example sentence: *The young ~ bowed to his sensei.*

136.

Diacritical pronunciation: \ thēˈäsəfē \
Phonetic pronunciation: thee-AH-suh-fee
Word origin: This word is made up of Greek parts.
Part of speech: noun
Definition: a collection of doctrine seeking knowledge of mysteries related to deity, cosmos, and self.
Example sentence: *Those interested in ~ seek to understand the mysteries of the universe and the bonds that unite the human and the divine.*

137.

Diacritical pronunciation: \ ˌyäkiˈtȯrē \
Phonetic pronunciation: yah-ki-TOR-ee
Word origin: This word is from Japanese.
Part of speech: noun
Definition: a Japanese dish of grilled meat on skewers.
Example sentence: *The hostess kindly informed the young patrons that the ~ was for eating, and not for reenacting the battle between Rey and Kylo Ren in "Episode VII."*

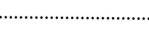

138.

Diacritical pronunciation: \ ˌkwädrəjəˈnarēəs \
Phonetic pronunciation: kwad-ruh-juh-NAYR-ee-us
Word origin: This word is from Latin.
Part of speech: adjective
Definition: being between 40 and 49 years old.
Example sentence: *The 34-year-old robber was so dispirited at being identified by witnesses as ~ that he decided to turn himself in.*

139.

Diacritical pronunciation: \ nōˈlishən \
Phonetic pronunciation: noh-LISH-un
Word origin: This word is probably from a Latin-derived French word.
Part of speech: noun
Definition: unwillingness.
Example sentence: *After asking for volunteers to clean up the campsite, Jordan frowned at the campers' universal ~.*

140.

Diacritical pronunciation: \ ˈflamˌbō \
Phonetic pronunciation: FLAM-boh
Word origin: This word is from a French word.
Part of speech: noun
Definition: a flaming torch.
Example sentence: *A procession of athletes marched into the stadium, each of them bearing a ~.*

141.

Diacritical pronunciation: \ ˌsərkəmˈvaˌlāt \
Phonetic pronunciation: sur-kum-VAL-ayt
Word origin: This word is from Latin.
Part of speech: adjective
Definition: surrounded by a rampart.
Example sentence: *The walls of the ~ city of Jericho were originally constructed for flood control.*

142.

Diacritical pronunciation: \ ˌanthrəpəˈsentrik \
Phonetic pronunciation: an-thruh-puh-SEN-trik
Word origin: This word is made up of originally Greek parts.
Part of speech: adjective
Definition: considering humans to be the most important things in the world.
Example sentence: *Billy complained that his father's rule that the dogs had to sleep outside at night was far too ~.*

143.

Diacritical pronunciation: \ ˈraptəs \
Phonetic pronunciation: RAP-tus
Word origin: This word is from Latin.
Part of speech: noun
Definition: a state of intense excitement.
Example sentence: *The painting depicted a saint looking heavenward in ~.*

144.

Diacritical pronunciation: \ fləˈjishəs \
Phonetic pronunciation: fluh-JISH-us
Word origin: This word is from Latin.
Part of speech: adjective
Definition: scandalous, wicked, or corrupt.
Example sentence: *The soldier's ~ deed resulted in his being dishonorably discharged from the army.*

145.

Diacritical pronunciation: \ bak͵tirēəˈlitik \
Phonetic pronunciation: bak-teer-ee-uh-LIT-ik
Word origin: This word is from a word that went from Greek to Latin.
Part of speech: adjective
Definition: relating to the destruction of bacteria.
Example sentence: *The ~ power of white blood cells helps the body overcome many diseases.*

146.

Diacritical pronunciation: \ ͵sapəˈnāshəs \
Phonetic pronunciation: sap-uh-NAY-shus
Word origin: This word is made up of a Latin part of Germanic origin plus a Latin part.
Part of speech: adjective
Definition: soapy.
Example sentence: *Talc and soapstone have a ~ feel.*

147.

Diacritical pronunciation: \ ˌvərˈtijəˌnāt \
Phonetic pronunciation: vur-TIJ-uh-nayt
Word origin: This word is from Latin.
Part of speech: verb
Definition: to spin around.
Example sentence: *Young children who ~ until they fall down are performing a rite of childhood.*

148.

Diacritical pronunciation: \ siˈnesᵊnt \
Phonetic pronunciation: si-NES-unt
Word origin: This word is from Latin.
Part of speech: adjective
Definition: getting older.
Example sentence: *Valerie warned Lars that ~ or not, she could still beat him in Scrabble, chess, and arm wrestling.*

149.

Diacritical pronunciation: \ ˈkän(t)swiˌtüd \

Phonetic pronunciation: KAHN(T)-swi-tood

Word origin: This word is from Latin.

Part of speech: noun

Definition: custom or habit.

Example sentence: *Dylan got in trouble for convincing his visiting cousin that the ~ in his city was to say hello by sticking your fingers up your nose.*

150.

Diacritical pronunciation: \ ˈpinəˌped \

Phonetic pronunciation: PIN-uh-ped

Word origin: This word is from Latin.

Part of speech: noun

Definition: a fin-footed aquatic carnivorous mammal, such as a seal or a walrus.

Example sentence: *Although the ~ finds its food in the sea, it needs to be on land or ice to give birth to its young.*

151.

Diacritical pronunciation: \ ä'bəmbrənt \
Phonetic pronunciation: ah-BUM-brunt
Word origin: This word is from Latin.
Part of speech: adjective
Definition: overhanging.
Example sentence: *Mira was leery of the ~ rocks on the cliffs above the path, but Richard wanted to picnic in their shade.*

152.

Diacritical pronunciation: \ rə'sōl \
Phonetic pronunciation: ri-SOHL
Word origin: This word came from French, which formed it from a Latin word.
Part of speech: noun
Definition: minced meat or fish covered with pastry and deep-fried.
Example sentence: *"I wish ~-flavored ice cream existed," said nobody, ever.*

153.

Diacritical pronunciation: \ flə'vesᵊnt \
Phonetic pronunciation: fluh-VES-unt
Word origin: This word is from Latin.
Part of speech: adjective
Definition: turning yellow.
Example sentence: *Kara enjoyed watching the ~ peacock fish swim in its large aquarium.*

154.

Diacritical pronunciation: \ ˌābēˌsē'darēəs \
Phonetic pronunciation: ay-bee-see-DAYR-ee-us
Word origin: This word is from Latin.
Part of speech: noun
Definition: a poem in which the lines begin with the letters of the alphabet in order.
Example sentence: *The teacher used an ~ about animals to teach kindergartners the alphabet.*

155.

Diacritical pronunciation: \ kə'lijənəs \
Phonetic pronunciation: kuh-LIJ-uh-nus
Word origin: This word is originally Latin, and probably went through French before becoming English.
Part of speech: adjective
Definition: dark and misty.
Example sentence: *A ~ sky presaged the approaching storm.*

156.

Diacritical pronunciation: \ 'embələs \
Phonetic pronunciation: EM-buh-lus
Word origin: This word went from Greek to Latin.
Part of speech: noun
Definition: a foreign or abnormal particle in the blood.
Example sentence: *Troy's grandfather had emergency surgery to remove an ~ from his right lung.*

157.

Diacritical pronunciation: \ ˈhȯˌbərk \

Phonetic pronunciation: HAH-burk

Word origin: This word is from an originally Germanic word that became French before becoming English.

Part of speech: noun

Definition: a long tunic made of ring or chain mail that was used as defensive armor in the 12th to 14th centuries.

Example sentence: *The sound of his ~ in the dryer kept Lucas up for hours.*

158.

Diacritical pronunciation: \ ˈbərklēəm \

Phonetic pronunciation: BURK-lee-um

Word origin: This word is from an American place name.

Part of speech: noun

Definition: a radioactive metallic element discovered by bombarding americium-241 with helium ions.

Example sentence: *~ was the fifth transuranic element to be discovered after neptunium, plutonium, curium, and americium.*

159.

Diacritical pronunciation: \ ˌkinəˈtōsəs \
Phonetic pronunciation: kin-uh-TOH-sis
Word origin: This word is from a word that went from Greek to Latin.
Part of speech: noun
Definition: motion sickness characterized by nausea.
Example sentence: *Melanie's date told her he would sweep her off her feet, but Melanie suspected that would induce ~.*

160.

Diacritical pronunciation: \ pəˈrīəˌsȯr \
Phonetic pronunciation: puh-RAHY-uh-sor
Word origin: This word is from Greek.
Part of speech: noun
Definition: a member of a family of Permian terrestrial reptiles.
Example sentence: *Paleontologists have proposed that the armor-plated ~ was an ancestor of turtles.*

161.

Diacritical pronunciation: \ chü'bä₁skō \

Phonetic pronunciation: choo-BAH-skoh

Word origin: This word is from a word that went from Latin to Portuguese to Spanish.

Part of speech: noun

Definition: a severe storm with rain and wind especially along the west coast of Central America.

Example sentence: *Jorge's comb-over was ravaged by the ~.*

162.

Diacritical pronunciation: \ ₁sīə'litik \

Phonetic pronunciation: sahy-uh-LIT-ik

Word origin: This word is from an originally Greek word that passed into Latin.

Part of speech: adjective

Definition: dispersing or driving out shadows.

Example sentence: *After a long night of ghost stories, Erma welcomed the ~ dawn.*

163.

Diacritical pronunciation: \ ˌintərˈpeˌlāt \
Phonetic pronunciation: in-tur-PEL-ayt
Word origin: This word is from Latin.
Part of speech: verb
Definition: to question formally about a governmental policy.
Example sentence: *At the next student government meeting, the students will ~ Sue the lunch lady about the sudden disappearance of Taco Tuesday.*

164.

Diacritical pronunciation: \ thrāˈsänəkəl \
Phonetic pronunciation: thray-SAHN-i-kul
Word origin: This word is from a Roman literary name.
Part of speech: adjective
Definition: bragging : boastful.
Example sentence: *As she watched her brother fall face-first into a muddy snowbank, Karla silently hoped this would make him less ~ about his skiing skills.*

165.

Diacritical pronunciation: \ ˈpȯrpərət \
Phonetic pronunciation: POR-puh-rit
Word origin: Originally Latin, this word went through Italian before becoming English.
Part of speech: adjective
Definition: clad in purple.
Example sentence: *Pete was excited to join his ~ pals sitting in the end zone at the Minnesota Vikings game.*

166.

Diacritical pronunciation: \ ˈbəkəl \
Phonetic pronunciation: BUH-kul
Word origin: The first part of this word is from an originally Latin word, and the second part is an English combining form.
Part of speech: adjective
Definition: relating to the cheeks.
Example sentence: *The diagram clearly showed the ~ salivary glands near the cheek muscle.*

167.

Diacritical pronunciation: \ əˈkrädrəməs \
Phonetic pronunciation: uh-KRAH-druh-mus
Word origin: This word is made up of Greek parts.
Part of speech: adjective
Definition: running to a point — used to describe a leaf in which the veins end at the tip.
Example sentence: *The leaves of the jujube and lotus exhibit ~ venation.*

168.

Diacritical pronunciation: \ ˌhespəˈridēəm \
Phonetic pronunciation: hes-puh-RID-ee-um
Word origin: This word went from Greek to Latin.
Part of speech: noun
Definition: a fruit with a leathery rind.
Example sentence: *Gil enjoyed a delicious ~ every morning of his vacation in Costa Rica.*

169.

Diacritical pronunciation: \ klen'dyüsətē \

Phonetic pronunciation: klen-DYOO-suh-tee

Word origin: This word is from Greek.

Part of speech: noun

Definition: the ability in a plant to escape disease.

Example sentence: *The plant's thick cuticle is largely responsible for its ~.*

170.

Diacritical pronunciation: \ ˌparə'limnēän \

Phonetic pronunciation: par-uh-LIM-nee-ahn

Word origin: This word was formed in Latin from Greek parts before becoming English.

Part of speech: noun

Definition: the portion of a lake extending from the shoreline to the deepest limit of rooted vegetation.

Example sentence: *Timothy swam out past the ~ to avoid swimming among the reeds and algae.*

171.

Diacritical pronunciation: \ ˈləvət \
Phonetic pronunciation: LUH-vut
Word origin: This word is probably from a Scottish geographical name.
Part of speech: noun
Definition: a mostly dusty green color mixture in fabrics originally intended to blend with the Scottish landscape.
Example sentence: *Jude's new tweed waistcoat in ~ looks just right with his Gordon Dress tartan.*

172.

Diacritical pronunciation: \ fləˈbeləˌfòrm \
Phonetic pronunciation: fluh-BEL-uh-form
Word origin: This word is made up of Latin parts.
Part of speech: adjective
Definition: shaped like a fan.
Example sentence: *One of the notable characteristics of the ginkgo tree is the ~ shape of its leaves.*

173.

Diacritical pronunciation: \ ˈsī͵fāt \

Phonetic pronunciation: SAHY-fayt

Word origin: This word is from a Greek element and an English combining form.

Part of speech: adjective

Definition: shaped like a cup.

Example sentence: *Nicholas asked the barista for an extra ~ receptacle, but merely got a blank stare.*

174.

Diacritical pronunciation: \ ˈwüts \

Phonetic pronunciation: woots

Word origin: This word is probably an alteration of a word from Kanarese, a South Indian language.

Part of speech: noun

Definition: a steel made anciently in India in small crucibles according to the oldest known process.

Example sentence: *Swords made from ~ were famous for their sharp, durable blades.*

175.

Diacritical pronunciation: \ ˈsilēəm \
Phonetic pronunciation: SIL-ee-um
Word origin: This word is from Greek.
Part of speech: noun
Definition: a plantain with seeds that become gelatinous when moist and that are used as a mild laxative.
Example sentence: *When a laxative is needed, health professionals may recommend products that contain ~, a natural fiber.*

176.

Diacritical pronunciation: \ ˈtīē \
Phonetic pronunciation: TAHY-ee
Word origin: This word is from Chinook.
Part of speech: noun
Definition: a king or chinook salmon especially when large.
Example sentence: *The ~ had to admit, there were moments when the whole "swimming upstream" thing didn't make a lot of sense to him.*

177.

Diacritical pronunciation: \ pō'pyet \

Phonetic pronunciation: poh-PYET

Word origin: This word went from Latin to Italian to French.

Part of speech: noun

Definition: a thin slice of meat or fish wrapped around a filling.

Example sentence: *Carol enjoyed the restaurant's entrée of a lamb ~ stuffed with pork, onions, and peppers.*

178.

Diacritical pronunciation: \ hȯr'nädə \

Phonetic pronunciation: hor-NAH-duh

Word origin: This word is from a word that went from Latin to Old Provençal to Spanish.

Part of speech: noun

Definition: a difficult usually one-day journey across a desert.

Example sentence: *The travelers almost perished for lack of water on the grim ~.*

179.

Diacritical pronunciation: \ gē'ō \
Phonetic pronunciation: gee-OH
Word origin: This word is from a Swiss name.
Part of speech: noun
Definition: a flat-topped undersea mountain, commonly found in the Pacific Ocean.
Example sentence: *The ship's sensors have recorded a ~ rising about 1,000 feet above the seabed.*

180.

Diacritical pronunciation: \ ō'sipədē \
Phonetic pronunciation: oh-SIP-uh-dee
Word origin: This word is from Greek.
Part of speech: noun
Definition: a square-bodied, long-legged, swift-running crab that lives in holes in the sand.
Example sentence: *The ~ can be found along sandy beaches from the northeastern United States to Brazil.*

181.

Diacritical pronunciation: \ rəˈfal \
Phonetic pronunciation: ruh-FAL
Word origin: This word is from a French word.
Part of speech: noun
Definition: a burst of artillery fire consisting of several rounds discharged as rapidly as possible from each gun.
Example sentence: *A ~ by the artillery battery kept the enemy infantry at bay.*

182.

Diacritical pronunciation: \ əˈlishēəm \
Phonetic pronunciation: i-LISH-ee-um
Word origin: This word is from Latin.
Part of speech: noun
Definition: a complex tentacle coming from the upper lip of a pediculate fish that serves as a lure to attract other fish.
Example sentence: *John explained his good fortune in this life by saying that in the last one he had been a tiny fish lured into an anglerfish's jaws by an ~.*

183.

Diacritical pronunciation: \ də'skrāzhə \

Phonetic pronunciation: di-SKRAY-zhuh

Word origin: This word was formed in Greek and went through Latin before becoming English.

Part of speech: noun

Definition: an abnormal condition of the body.

Example sentence: *In her research on medical history, Georgette encountered a number of records mentioning the vague diagnosis of ~.*

184.

Diacritical pronunciation: \ ˌkampə'nyòl \

Phonetic pronunciation: kam-puh-NYOHL

Word origin: This word is from French.

Part of speech: noun

Definition: the European field vole.

Example sentence: *The ~ is sometimes mistaken for the Eurasian harvest mouse.*

185.

Diacritical pronunciation: \ pōsh'wär \

Phonetic pronunciation: pohsh-WAHR

Word origin: This word is from French, which ultimately took it from a word of Germanic origin.

Part of speech: noun

Definition: a stencil process for making colored prints or adding color to a printed key illustration.

Example sentence: *The use of ~ was especially popular in illustrating French fashion journals of the 1920s.*

186.

Diacritical pronunciation: \ ˈliktənˌstīn \

Phonetic pronunciation: LIK-tun-stahyn

Word origin: This word is from a central European geographical name.

Part of speech: adjective

Definition: of or from the principality of the same name.

Example sentence: *~ companies produce textiles, pharmaceuticals, and precision instruments.*

187.

Diacritical pronunciation: \ pē'kər \
Phonetic pronunciation: pee-KUR
Word origin: This word is from French.
Part of speech: noun
Definition: an attendant directing the hounds in a hunt.
Example sentence: *The ~ sounded one long blast on his hunting horn.*

188.

Diacritical pronunciation: \ wä'tō \
Phonetic pronunciation: wah-TOH
Word origin: This word is from a French name.
Part of speech: noun
Definition: a hat with a shallow crown and a wide brim that turns up in the back to hold flowers.
Example sentence: *There was a year in middle school when Lianne toyed with making the ~ her signature accessory before settling on the turtleneck sweater.*

189.

Diacritical pronunciation: \ ˌrīnəˈrājə \
Phonetic pronunciation: rhahy-nuh-RAY-juh
Word origin: This word was formed in Latin from Greek parts before becoming English.
Part of speech: noun
Definition: nosebleed.
Example sentence: *Claire attempted to fake a ~ in order to get out of taking her math test, but her plan failed when the teacher saw a bottle of ketchup peeking out of her backpack.*

190.

Diacritical pronunciation: \ pāˈsän(ˌ)tā \
Phonetic pronunciation: pay-SAHN-tay
Word origin: This word went from Latin to Italian.
Part of speech: adverb
Definition: in a heavy manner — used as a direction in music.
Example sentence: *The dancers were not sure how best to interpret the section of "The Firebird" that is played molto ~.*

191.

Diacritical pronunciation: \ ˌheləˈkrīsəm \

Phonetic pronunciation: hel-uh-KRAHY-sum

Word origin: This word is from Greek.

Part of speech: noun

Definition: an African and Australian plant with shining flower heads which retain their color when dried.

Example sentence: *Martha made a wreath of the dried, brightly colored flowers of the ~.*

192.

Diacritical pronunciation: \ kwäˈdrīgə \

Phonetic pronunciation: kwah-DRAHY-guh

Word origin: This word is from Latin.

Part of speech: noun

Definition: an ancient Roman chariot drawn by four horses.

Example sentence: *For his birthday Anapaum asked his parents for a ~, but instead he got a sit-down conversation on humility.*

193.

Diacritical pronunciation: \ ˌaˌküshˈmäⁿ \
Phonetic pronunciation: a-koosh-MAHN
Word origin: This word is from a French word.
Part of speech: noun
Definition: the state during and after childbirth.
Example sentence: *Maggie's parents promised to take care of her other children during ~.*

194.

Diacritical pronunciation: \ ˌipsēˈdiksətˌizəm \
Phonetic pronunciation: ip-see-DIK-sit-iz-um
Word origin: This word is from Latin.
Part of speech: noun
Definition: dogmatic assertiveness.
Example sentence: *Martine's ~ tired her friends and put off strangers.*

195.

Diacritical pronunciation: \ ˌsiprəˈpēdēəm \
Phonetic pronunciation: sip-ri-PEED-ee-um
Word origin: This word is from Greek-derived Latin.
Part of speech: noun
Definition: an orchid with large, showily colored or marked flowers with a lip that forms a pouch.
Example sentence: *The flower of the ~ somewhat resembles a lady's slipper.*

196.

Diacritical pronunciation: \ ˌkerəˈtäjənəs \
Phonetic pronunciation: kayr-uh-TAH-juh-nus
Word origin: This word is made up of Greek parts plus an English combining form.
Part of speech: adjective
Definition: producing horn or hornlike tissue.
Example sentence: *A horse's hoof is composed of ~ material.*

197.

Diacritical pronunciation: \ ˌbätòˈnyā \

Phonetic pronunciation: bah-toh-NYAY

Word origin: This word is from French.

Part of speech: noun

Definition: the chief of the advocates of a court.

Example sentence: *The ~ is responsible for deciding appeals against the bar.*

198.

Diacritical pronunciation: \ ˌpentəˈkästəs \

Phonetic pronunciation: pen-tuh-KAHS-tis

Word origin: This word is from Greek.

Part of speech: noun

Definition: a troop of 50 soldiers in the Spartan army.

Example sentence: *A ~ was sent to guard the bridge to prevent the enemy's entry into the city.*

199.

Diacritical pronunciation: \ ˌsōləˈnäɡləfəs \
Phonetic pronunciation: soh-luh-NAH-gluh-fus
Word origin: This word is made up of two Greek parts plus an English combining form.
Part of speech: adjective
Definition: having tubular fangs that can be raised to an upright position.
Example sentence: *Vipers belong to the family of ~ snakes.*

200.

Diacritical pronunciation: \ rāˈzō \
Phonetic pronunciation: ray-ZOH
Word origin: This word came from French, which formed it from a Latin word.
Part of speech: noun
Definition: a group of meteorological stations under common direction or with a common purpose.
Example sentence: *The ~ indicated that the brunt of the storm would hit around three o'clock.*

201.

Diacritical pronunciation: \ ˈlirə͵pīp \

Phonetic pronunciation: LIR-uh-pahyp

Word origin: This word is from Latin.

Part of speech: noun

Definition: a long cloth attached to a medieval round stuffed head covering.

Example sentence: *The organizers of the Renaissance Fair announced that they would not pay for Becky's tie-dye ~; nay, not a farthing.*

202.

Diacritical pronunciation: \ ˈfremətəs \

Phonetic pronunciation: FREM-uh-tus

Word origin: This word is from Latin.

Part of speech: noun

Definition: a sensation felt in a part of the body that vibrates during speech.

Example sentence: *While the patient was speaking, the doctor placed his hand over each part of the patient's chest to evaluate the ~ it produced.*

203.

Diacritical pronunciation: \ neˈfrȯrəfē \

Phonetic pronunciation: ne-FROR-uh-fee

Word origin: This word is from Greek.

Part of speech: noun

Definition: the suturing of a floating kidney to the posterior abdominal wall.

Example sentence: *The surgeon treated Amy's wandering kidney by performing a ~.*

204.

Diacritical pronunciation: \ bləˈmänj \

Phonetic pronunciation: bluh-MAHNJ

Word origin: This word came from an originally French word plus an originally Latin word that became French.

Part of speech: noun

Definition: a molded dessert made from gelatinous or starchy substances and sweetened, flavored milk.

Example sentence: *No one at the potluck dinner wanted to try Kelly's dessert, ~ in the shape of a snake eating a fish.*

205.

Diacritical pronunciation: \ ə'nastrə(ˌ)fē \
Phonetic pronunciation: uh-NAS-truh-fee
Word origin: This word passed from Greek to Latin.
Part of speech: noun
Definition: inversion of the usual order of words in a sentence for rhetorical effect.
Example sentence: *Friends of Yoda often report that after a few days, the novelty of his ~ wears off, and annoying it becomes.*

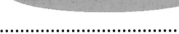

206.

Diacritical pronunciation: \ 'tiləˌpäd \
Phonetic pronunciation: TIL-uh-pahd
Word origin: Both parts of this word are originally Greek.
Part of speech: adjective
Definition: having feathered feet.
Example sentence: *Many owl species are ~.*

207.

Diacritical pronunciation: \ ˈmänchər \
Phonetic pronunciation: MAHN-chur
Word origin: This word is from a French word.
Part of speech: noun
Definition: a setting for a jewel.
Example sentence: *The diamond's ~ was platinum, but the band was gold.*

208.

Diacritical pronunciation: \ ˌhīpəˈräzmēə \
Phonetic pronunciation: hahy-puh-RAHZ-mee-uh
Word origin: This word is made up of originally Greek parts.
Part of speech: noun
Definition: an extremely strong sense of smell.
Example sentence: *Lauren's ~ makes it difficult for her to be around smokers.*

209.

Diacritical pronunciation: \ ˈdithəˌram \
Phonetic pronunciation: DITH-i-ram
Word origin: This word is from Greek.
Part of speech: noun
Definition: a statement or piece of writing in an exalted, impassioned style usually featuring praise.
Example sentence: *The chorus launched into a ~ in praise of Dionysus, the Greek god of wine, fertility, and drama.*

210.

Diacritical pronunciation: \ vōˈleməˌtȯl \
Phonetic pronunciation: voh-LEM-uh-tahl
Word origin: This word was formed from an originally Latin part and an English combining form.
Part of speech: noun
Definition: a slightly sweet crystalline alcohol found especially in a certain species of mushroom.
Example sentence: *~ is a natural sweetening agent that can be used in place of sugar.*

211.

Diacritical pronunciation: \ ˈsämə \
Phonetic pronunciation: SAH-muh
Word origin: This word came from Italian, which formed it from a Latin word.
Part of speech: noun
Definition: the rim of a volcanic crater.
Example sentence: *The Jackson family visited the ~ of Mount Vesuvius and took video of the fumes rising from the caldera.*

212.

Diacritical pronunciation: \ ēˈkäfərəd \
Phonetic pronunciation: ee-KAH-fuh-rid
Word origin: This word is made up of originally Greek parts.
Part of speech: noun
Definition: a small moth whose larvae feed on leaves and flowers.
Example sentence: *Florence noticed a brown ~ on one of the roses she was about to pick.*

213.

Diacritical pronunciation: \ ˌtsvitəˈrīən \

Phonetic pronunciation: tsvit-uh-RAHY-un

Word origin: This word is made up of a German part plus a Greek part.

Part of speech: noun

Definition: a dipolar ion.

Example sentence: *A ~ is a neutral molecule with a positive and a negative charge at different locations within it.*

214.

Diacritical pronunciation: \ ˈnanēˌgī \

Phonetic pronunciation: NAN-ee-gahy

Word origin: This word is from a native Australian name.

Part of speech: noun

Definition: a red, iridescent Australian food fish.

Example sentence: *While Edna was visiting New South Wales, she had her first taste of ~.*

215.

Diacritical pronunciation: \ ˈyügənt͵shtēl \
Phonetic pronunciation: YOO-gunt-shteel
Word origin: This word is from German.
Part of speech: noun
Definition: a late 19th-century and early 20th-century German decorative style.
Example sentence: *Nick's favorite exhibit at the Los Angeles County Museum of Art is the Art Nouveau and ~ wing.*

216.

Diacritical pronunciation: \ əˈkimē͵īn \
Phonetic pronunciation: uh-KIM-ee-ahyn
Word origin: This word consists of originally Greek parts that passed into Latin plus an English combining form.
Part of speech: adjective
Definition: of or relating to a genus of rodents of South and Central America that includes various spiny rats.
Example sentence: *The zoologist classified the hedgehog rat as an ~ rodent.*

217.

Diacritical pronunciation: \ ˈdipnəwəs \
Phonetic pronunciation: DIP-nuh-wus
Word origin: Both parts of this word are originally Greek.
Part of speech: adjective
Definition: having both lungs and gills.
Example sentence: *Frogs are ~ for a time during their development, but as adults have lungs only.*

218.

Diacritical pronunciation: \ ˌbüˌlü'tirēˌän \
Phonetic pronunciation: boo-loo-TEE-ree-ahn
Word origin: This word is from Greek.
Part of speech: noun
Definition: an ancient Greek council chamber.
Example sentence: *The ~ was a covered chamber fitted with banks of seats like a theater.*

219.

Diacritical pronunciation: \ dəˈgerəˌtīp \
Phonetic pronunciation: duh-GAYR-uh-tahyp
Word origin: This word is from a French name plus a part that went from Greek to French.
Part of speech: noun
Definition: a photograph produced on a silver plate.
Example sentence: *The ~ was popular from its invention in 1839 until 1860.*

220.

Diacritical pronunciation: \ ˈrirˌbrās \
Phonetic pronunciation: REER-brays
Word origin: This word is from English.
Part of speech: noun
Definition: plate armor for the upper arm.
Example sentence: *Emile swung his sword and struck his foe on the left ~.*

221.

Diacritical pronunciation: \ tə'bùr(ˌ)bü \

Phonetic pronunciation: ti-BOOR-boo

Word origin: This word went from Galibi, an Amerindian language, to French.

Part of speech: noun

Definition: a tropical American tree with yellowish flowers and very light wood.

Example sentence: *Fishermen along the coast of Brazil use small boats made from the wood of the ~.*

222.

Diacritical pronunciation: \ 'süjē \

Phonetic pronunciation: SOO-jee

Word origin: This word is perhaps from Japanese.

Part of speech: verb

Definition: to wash down (as the deck of a ship).

Example sentence: *The crew found it particularly annoying when every time the captain ordered them to ~ the deck, Isaac quickly yelled, "Not it."*

223.

Diacritical pronunciation: \ ˈverˌmäkt \
Phonetic pronunciation: VAYR-mahkt
Word origin: This word consists of two German elements.
Part of speech: noun
Definition: the armed forces especially of Germany from 1935 to 1945.
Example sentence: *Some high-ranking members of the ~ tried to assassinate Hitler in 1944 but failed and were executed.*

224.

Diacritical pronunciation: \ gloˈkäthəˌwē \
Phonetic pronunciation: glah-KAH-thuh-wee
Word origin: This word is from Latin or Greek.
Part of speech: noun
Definition: a young hermit crab that is beyond the swimming larval stages.
Example sentence: *The ~ grows to about two inches long and lives curled up inside an empty snail shell.*

225.

Diacritical pronunciation: \ bäkˈshīsh \
Phonetic pronunciation: bahk-SHAHY-sh
Word origin: This word is from an Iranian geographical name.
Part of speech: noun
Definition: a Persian carpet with angular designs.
Example sentence: *Sophia received many compliments on the newly acquired ~ on her living room floor.*

226.

Diacritical pronunciation: \ səˈlālē \
Phonetic pronunciation: suh-LAY-lee
Word origin: This word is from Samoan.
Part of speech: noun
Definition: a small, dusky silver or silvery bronze fish widely distributed in the tropical Indo-Pacific area.
Example sentence: *While fishing in a river in Hawaii, Chris caught a 10-inch ~.*

227.

Diacritical pronunciation: \ gə'lärdēə \
Phonetic pronunciation: guh-LAHR-dee-uh
Word origin: This word is from a French name.
Part of speech: noun
Definition: a plant with hairy leaves and long, stalked flower heads.
Example sentence: *The ~ has bright yellow blooms.*

228.

Diacritical pronunciation: \ kə'rò(ˌ)chō \
Phonetic pronunciation: kuh-RAH-choh
Word origin: This word is from Italian.
Part of speech: noun
Definition: a large wheeled vehicle used in medieval Italy as a rallying point for battling army.
Example sentence: *Before the battle, the soldiers gathered round the ~ for a stirring speech from their commander.*

229.

Diacritical pronunciation: \ ˌyäkəˈpevər \

Phonetic pronunciation: yah-kuh-PEV-ur

Word origin: This word is from Afrikaans, which probably formed it from a Dutch name.

Part of speech: noun

Definition: any of several large-eyed reddish food fishes of southern Africa.

Example sentence: *While visiting Cape Town, Janice enjoyed a meal of filleted and fried ~.*

230.

Diacritical pronunciation: \ səmˈskärə \

Phonetic pronunciation: sum-SKAH-ruh

Word origin: This word is from Sanskrit.

Part of speech: noun

Definition: a Hindu ceremony of purification.

Example sentence: *The ~ of naming a newborn Hindu child traditionally takes place on the 11th day after the birth.*

231.

Diacritical pronunciation: \ ˌvəlˈseləm \
Phonetic pronunciation: vul-SEL-um
Word origin: This word is from Latin.
Part of speech: noun
Definition: a surgical forceps with serrated, clawed, or hooked blades.
Example sentence: *Henry was forced to rethink medicine as his career path when the sight of the ~ made him pass out cold.*

....

232.

Diacritical pronunciation: \ ˌperseˈäd \
Phonetic pronunciation: payr-see-AHD
Word origin: This word is from a French word.
Part of speech: adjective
Definition: garnished with or containing parsley.
Example sentence: *Marina decided to try out the recipe for baked mussels ~.*

233.

Diacritical pronunciation: \ ˌfȯrməˈtō(ˌ)rā \
Phonetic pronunciation: for-muh-TOH-ray
Word origin: This word went from Latin to Italian.
Part of speech: noun
Definition: a molder or modeler.
Example sentence: *Byron enjoyed his work as a ~ of plaster architectural models.*

234.

Diacritical pronunciation: \ ˈäyərˌvādə \
Phonetic pronunciation: ah-yur-VAY-duh
Word origin: This word is from Sanskrit.
Part of speech: noun
Definition: the traditional Hindu system of medicine based largely on homeopathy and naturopathy.
Example sentence: *In ~, deer horns can be used in preparations to treat respiratory infections.*

235.

Diacritical pronunciation: \ 'brü͵hä \
Phonetic pronunciation: BROO-hah
Word origin: This word is from Spanish.
Part of speech: noun
Definition: a witch or sorceress.
Example sentence: *After hearing his grandmother's story about the ~, Antonio decided it might be best to sleep with the lights on for the rest of his life.*

236.

Diacritical pronunciation: \ 'nägəl͵flü \
Phonetic pronunciation: NAH-gul-floo
Word origin: This word is from German.
Part of speech: noun
Definition: a massive variegated conglomerate in the Alps.
Example sentence: *Geologists have found many fossils in a ~ in Switzerland.*

237.

Diacritical pronunciation: \ bō'mäntij \

Phonetic pronunciation: boh-MAHN-tij

Word origin: This word is of unknown origin.

Part of speech: noun

Definition: a substance to fill holes or cracks in wood or metal.

Example sentence: *Bart asked the conservator to replace all the old ~ in the bronze statuette.*

238.

Diacritical pronunciation: \ ˌstre(ˌ)fōˌsim'bōlēə \

Phonetic pronunciation: streh-foh-sim-BOH-lee-uh

Word origin: This word is from Greek.

Part of speech: noun

Definition: reversal or transposition of phrases, words, or letters or of any symbols especially in reading.

Example sentence: *Because of his ~, Ryan was diagnosed as having a learning disorder.*

239.

Diacritical pronunciation: \ ˌtərpˈsikə(ˌ)rē \
Phonetic pronunciation: turp-SIK-uh-ree
Word origin: This word is from a Greek name.
Part of speech: noun
Definition: dancing : choreography.
Example sentence: *The television show features couples exhibiting their skills in ~.*

240.

Diacritical pronunciation: \ ˈveltˌpōləˈtēk \
Phonetic pronunciation: VELT-poh-luh-teek
Word origin: This word consists of a German part plus a part that went from Greek to French to German.
Part of speech: noun
Definition: international politics.
Example sentence: *Kaiser Wilhelm II fostered Germany's ~ in his quest for power.*

241.

Diacritical pronunciation: \ rō'kī \
Phonetic pronunciation: roh-KAHY
Word origin: This word is from a French word.
Part of speech: noun
Definition: an 18th-century ornamental style characterized by artificial rockwork and pierced shellwork.
Example sentence: *Early 18th-century French fountains were often decorated in the style of ~.*

242.

Diacritical pronunciation: \ ˌərtə'karēə \
Phonetic pronunciation: urt-uh-KAYR-ee-uh
Word origin: This word was formed from a Latin word.
Part of speech: noun
Definition: hives.
Example sentence: *It took several weeks for Maureen to realize that her ~ was being caused by her new laundry detergent.*

243.

Diacritical pronunciation: \ ˌpanəˈshür \
Phonetic pronunciation: pan-uh-SHOOR
Word origin: This word is from French.
Part of speech: noun
Definition: mottling, specifically of other-colored spots with the normal green in foliage.
Example sentence: *Frances planted a spotted laurel with bright golden ~ near her kitchen window.*

244.

Diacritical pronunciation: \ kōˈkil \
Phonetic pronunciation: koh-KIL
Word origin: This word is from a French word.
Part of speech: noun
Definition: an artist's white drawing board with a stippled texture that produces a dotted drawing.
Example sentence: *For her sister's wedding gift, Emmy created a charcoal sketch on ~ board complete with a homemade pinewood frame.*

245.

Diacritical pronunciation: \ ˈtiksəs \
Phonetic pronunciation: TIK-sis
Word origin: This word went from Greek to Latin to English.
Part of speech: noun
Definition: the arrangement of a single leaf in the bud.
Example sentence: *One type of ~ in budding leaves is involute, with both margins folded inward, as in the water lily.*

246.

Diacritical pronunciation: \ təˈlähā \
Phonetic pronunciation: tuh-LAH-hay
Word origin: This word is from Spanish, which formed it from a Nahuatl word.
Part of speech: noun
Definition: a tick of the American tropics that infests horses, humans, and other mammals.
Example sentence: *After being bitten by a ~, Diego became ill with a high fever.*

247.

Diacritical pronunciation: \ fō'täfəgəs \
Phonetic pronunciation: foh-TAH-fuh-gus
Word origin: This word consists of two Greek parts plus an English combining form.
Part of speech: adjective
Definition: preferring or thriving in shade.
Example sentence: *Lots of people described Dan as a homebody, but he preferred to think of himself as ~.*

248.

Diacritical pronunciation: \ ˌhī(ˌ)pō'züksəs \
Phonetic pronunciation: hahy-poh-ZOOK-sis
Word origin: This word is from Greek.
Part of speech: noun
Definition: the use in a parallel construction of successive subject-verb clauses.
Example sentence: *The following sentence exemplifies ~: John sang, Jane laughed, and the dog howled.*

249.

Diacritical pronunciation: \ ˌram(p)fəˈthēkə \
Phonetic pronunciation: ram(p)fuh-THEE-kuh
Word origin: This word is made up of a Greek part and a part that went from Greek to Latin.
Part of speech: noun
Definition: the hornlike sheath of a bird's bill composed of modified scales.
Example sentence: *The ornithologist has been studying the development of the ~ in petrels and albatrosses.*

250.

Diacritical pronunciation: \ səˈfräsᵊn(ˌ)ē \
Phonetic pronunciation: suh-FRAH-suh-nee
Word origin: This word is from Greek.
Part of speech: noun
Definition: self-control, restraint, or prudence.
Example sentence: *Upon learning of Beyoncé's surprise album release, Amelia lost all ~ and let loose a euphoric scream from her cubicle.*